NLP

Efficient And Straightforward Neuro Linguistic Programming Techniques To Transform Your Life

(Acquire The Knowledge To Discern Non-Verbal Communication Through This All-Encompassing Manual)

Jamie Gledhill

TABLE OF CONTENT

What is Depression? 1

Beliefs And Outcomes 9

Managing Emotions through the Application of NLP Techniques in the Context of Travel Passengers 23

Comprehending the Fundamentals of the Neuro-Linguistic Programming Concept 30

Representational Systems 41

NLP Simplified 61

Transform states without resources into states with resources. 100

How Neuro-Linguistic Programming Works? 107

Guarding Against Manipulation 120

How to Keep Motivated 139

What is Depression?

Depression can be characterized as a state of overall despondency and retreat; a profound sadness that exceeds what can be reasonably justified by any objective rationale.

Clinical depression can be defined as an exceptionally severe form of depression that is considered abnormal, either due to a lack of evident external causes or an intensification and prolongation of the distress caused by unfortunate life circumstances, beyond what would typically be anticipated.

When observing an individual who appears to be experiencing depression, even in the absence of an official diagnosis, certain indicators may be evident, serving as potential cues to identify depressive symptoms in that person or within oneself. The aforementioned indicators comprise: The aforementioned signs and symptoms encompass: These manifestations encompass: These manifestations include:

• Contemplation of self-harm or possible acts of self-harm leading to suicide.

The individual exhibits difficulty in maintaining focus or reaching conclusive decisions. In certain instances, they may additionally encounter difficulty in recollecting specific particulars regarding select occurrences or circumstances that may bear significance in the future.

• They consistently experience feelings of sorrow, hollowness, or apprehension.

• They experience a reduction in energy levels and consistently exhibit fatigue.

• There persists a constant presence of discomfort, aching, cramping, or headaches.

- The individual experiences a sense of powerlessness or diminished self-worth.

- One may exhibit excessive eating or a decline in appetite

- Furthermore, individuals may experience a sense of despair or harbor a negative outlook on existence.

- Their former hobbies and interests, including sexual activities, no longer evoke any enthusiasm or passion.

- In the event that individuals do not experience any difficulty falling asleep, it is observed that they either rise early or tend to sleep for extended periods of time.

Similar to many aspects of existence, there exist various forms of depression that one must confront. Possible diagnoses may include atypical depression, major depression, situational depression, persistent depressive disorder, premenstrual dysphoric disorder, bipolar disorder, peripartum depression or postpartum depression, seasonal affective disorder, or even psychotic depression.

Every depression possesses distinct characteristics and will vary from the preceding one.

Major depression refers to a psychological state characterized by experiencing depressive symptoms for a significant portion of any given day, on a greater frequency than periods without such symptoms.

Persistent depressive disorder, also known as dysthymia in conjunction with chronic major depression, is characterized by a duration lasting two years or more.

Bipolar depression, commonly referred to as manic depression, manifests as a psychological condition characterized by alternating episodes of intense elation and profound sadness, significantly impacting an individual's behavioral patterns. The periods characterized by diminished emotional well-being in individuals experiencing depression are likely to exhibit indications of severe depressive symptoms.

Seasonal affective disorder, also known as SAD, manifests as depressive symptoms exclusively during specific seasons. This phenomenon predominantly occurs in the winter season, primarily due to the gradual reduction in daylight hours and decreased exposure to sunlight. Typically, it tends to dissipate prior to the arrival of summer or spring.

Psychotic depression typically manifests when individuals experience a severe depressive episode accompanied by psychotic manifestations.

Peripartum or postpartum depression occurs in the immediate aftermath of childbirth in women.

Premenstrual dysphoric disorder (PMDD) is characterized by the onset of depressive symptoms coinciding with the commencement of menstruation in women.

Situational depression refers to a condition wherein an individual encounters challenges in effectively coping with stress resulting from significant life events, such as bereavement or marital dissolution.

Atypical depression manifests when there is a specifier regarding the etiology of the depressive symptoms.

Several factors could exacerbate depression symptoms for the individual affected.

The administration of drugs or medications can potentially elicit adverse side effects in individuals who commence a new medication due to their unfamiliarity with the medication's effects. This phenomenon can also occur upon discontinuation of medication, as the body necessitates time to readapt. The use of illicit substances can also lead to the manifestation of depressive symptoms.

An individual who is experiencing physical illness or has prevalent medical conditions such as AIDS or cancer has the potential to exacerbate symptoms of depression. As the severity of the illness or condition increases, its impact on an individual's lifestyle similarly intensifies.

Endogenous shifts in hormonal activity are an inherent component of human physiology. Remarkably, they can act as catalysts for the development of depressive symptoms. These alterations will occur during periods of physiological transformation, such as adolescence or pregnancy.

The experience of grief or loss is highly subjective, but even situations that are generally perceived as positive, such as a marriage, can potentially lead to emotional upheaval.

The way in which one lives can engender medical conditions, contingent upon one's actions and the timing thereof. In instances where an individual leads a life fraught with heightened levels of stress or exhibits poor health, their susceptibility to the onset of depression is augmented.

Beliefs And Outcomes

"In the following chapter, you will acquire knowledge and understanding of:

Consequences

The 9-step inquiry model for organizing and advancing your desired outcome

The four fundamental inquiries for achieving the desired outcome.

☐ Convictions

☐ Convictions and Results – the three essential convictions required regarding your outcomes

Outcomes

What is an outcome? In essence, the outcome can be defined as the ultimate fulfillment of one's desires. In the realm of Neuro Linguistic Programming, the term 'outcome' pertains to the state that is sought after. The state that you aspire to attain is currently absent from your possession and is something you would like to acquire. Upon acquiring knowledge and recognition of one's intended condition, a tangible result is hence established. This result will assist you in strategizing your path from your current condition to your envisioned state.

Nevertheless, exercise caution in avoiding the confusion between task and outcome. In the realm of Neuro Linguistic Programming, the notions of task and outcome are inherently independent from one another. The desired outcome represents the state that you genuinely seek to achieve.

Conversely, a task is an activity undertaken with the purpose of attaining a desired result. Hence, refrain from undertaking any tasks until you possess a clearly defined set of outcomes. Alternatively, in the absence of taking the aforementioned course of action, one would incur an expenditure of financial resources, consume a significant amount of time, and expend considerable effort in engaging in said activity.

If you remain uncertain about determining your desired outcome, there exists an avenue for its development. This can be achieved by engaging in a process of introspection, wherein one poses inquiries related to specific aspirations that are perceived as attainable, inspiring, and grounded in reality. This is a matter that you are already aware of in your own being. The following are the outlined inquiries comprising a 9-step guide designed to assist you in formulating and cultivating the desired outcome that resonates with you.

What do you want?

How will you determine whether you have attained your desired outcome? How can one determine the accomplishment of one's objectives?

May I inquire as to the details of the location, timing, and company involved?

Where would you prefer the result to be located? (place)

When would you prefer to have the result? (time or deadline)

With whom do you desire the result? (an individual or collective entity with whom you desire to communicate your achievements)

What available resources do you possess that can aid you in attaining your intended result?

These categories may encompass individuals and acquaintances, tangible items, individual attributes and credentials, material possessions and influential figures.

Are you able to sustain this result?

What are the potential ramifications if this outcome is successfully attained?

Does the desired result align with your core identity?

How do your results align to form a unified and cohesive entirety?

Action plan

What actions should I take?

Once you have formulated a desired outcome or a series of outcomes, it is now imperative to consider the strategic means by which they can be effectively realized. The four fundamental inquiries that one must ponder each time they strive for success in achieving their desired outcome are as follows:

What is my truest and deepest longing?

This denotes the state or desired result that you have formulated.

What are the reasons behind my desire for this?

What factors drive and inspire you in your pursuit of this particular outcome? To what extent do you desire it? What are the ingrained values that have influenced your desire for this particular outcome?

This will serve to instill a sense of inspiration and motivation within you, particularly in moments when you lack the inclination to proceed with the necessary actions towards reaching your intended state or desired outcome.

What would be the method of transportation to arrive at the destination?

What specific actions can you undertake to effectively accomplish the desired outcome you truly seek?

This pertains to the tactics that must be employed to achieve the desired result.

Whenever possible, construct the instructions in a systematic manner to facilitate your comprehension and execution.

In the event of any unforeseen circumstances, what would be the course of action?

What are the potential hazards associated with the pursuit of my desired state and outcome?

In the event of a failure of my concrete steps, what course of action ought I to undertake?

What alternative courses of action can I consider? In the event that my initial plan proves unsuccessful, what alternatives should be considered? Is it advisable to persist in my pursuit of the desired state or outcome if I encounter a setback at this current phase?

This pertains to your mitigation strategies and risk mitigation plans in relation to the pursuit of your desired state and outcome.

On a sheet of notebook paper, make note of the questions and your responses to these fundamental inquiries. By doing so, you will have a tangible resource to reference whenever you wish to reinforce the desired outcome in your mind.

Beliefs

Beliefs, in succinct terms, comprise the guiding principles that shape one's conduct and decisions. Your belief system shapes your cognitive frameworks. Mental models encompass the guiding principles that individuals employ for the purpose of effectively executing tasks. Furthermore, it encompasses your perception of the external environment, shaped by personal inclinations, abilities, and prior interactions in regard to individuals, interpersonal connections, locations, pursuits, objects, and circumstances. To put it differently, it can be said that your worldview is intricately influenced by your system of beliefs. The majority of individuals hold their belief system to be enigmatic and flawless, yet in actuality and reality, such systems are not without flaws.

In the majority of cases, your system of beliefs tends to become a self-fulfilling prophecy. As an illustration, in the event that you hold the belief that you possess a charismatic demeanor, there is an increased probability that you will engage with others in an uninhibited manner. Conversely, should you hold the belief that you are lacking in likability, your inclination to engage others openly will diminish. Hence, you exhibit timidity and apprehension.

In Neuro Linguistic Programming, beliefs can be understood as no more than presuppositions. This implies that convictions serve solely as guidelines for behavior, rather than being constituted as objective realities or verifiable truths. Advocates of Neuro Linguistic Programming assert that if your existing belief system fails to yield favorable outcomes in your life, it is imperative to modify them.

Convictions and Results – The 3 Essential Beliefs Regarding Your Outcomes

To achieve greater success in any endeavor you pursue, it is imperative to first ascertain your intended state or desired outcome. Subsequently, it is imperative to modify one's convictions in a manner that facilitates the attainability and reasonableness of the desired state or outcome. The sole method to achieve this goal is by consistently articulating the ensuing statements or regularly reaffirming them to oneself on a daily basis:

Attaining (your preferred state or outcome) is within the realm of possibility.

I possess the capability to attain (express your intended state or outcome)

I am entitled to attain (state your desired state or outcome).

Regarding the initial assertion, it acknowledges the veracity of the notion that attaining one's preferred condition or result is indeed attainable. Bear in mind that your limitations are unknown to you; therefore, it would be wise to push yourself towards the attainment of formidable aspirations. Keep in mind the adage that states, "One's true capabilities remain elusive until they fully tap into their potential." Assert with confidence that such achievement is, indeed, within reach.

Regarding the second statement, it acknowledges the veracity that you possess the capacity to attain your desired condition or result. For a significant number of individuals, underestimating their worth is an ingrained practice that originated during their childhood. Indeed, their mental state was consumed by pessimistic beliefs regarding the boundaries they had imposed upon themselves. Believe in your abilities and recognize that the mind's capacity to envision success aligns with the body's potential for accomplishment. It is imperative to avoid underestimating oneself by lacking belief in one's capabilities. Based on Henry Ford's statement, "Whether you believe you are capable or incapable, you are correct." Declare that you possess the capacity.

In regards to the third statement, it acknowledges the veracity of your entitlement to attain your desired condition or result. Maintain the conviction that you are worthy of attaining your objectives. Cultivate a strong sense of self-advocacy and self-appreciation. It is imperative to bear in mind that without self-belief, others will be unlikely to place their trust in you. Assert that you are entitled to it.

Managing Emotions through the Application of NLP Techniques in the Context of Travel Passengers

Emotions are merely choices, and there exist alternatives for effecting significant transformations. When emotions are regarded as choices rather than conditions to be tolerated. You are presented with the chance to exercise your agency in making determinations, and the impact it will have on your outcomes is contingent upon the level of dedication and effort you invest in honing these skills.

By attuning yourself to your emotions, you will augment your ability to retrace your steps and identify the specific visual or auditory stimulus that triggered the corresponding feeling. NLP can assist in effectively dealing with frustrations, irritations, and anxieties by cultivating a state of curiosity to explore the underlying reasons behind these emotions.

An inquisitive nature promotes the formation of novel neural connections. Aids in cognitive enhancement and fosters increased levels of involvement. By approaching an answer with a heightened sense of curiosity, one may observe the remarkable disappearance of numerous negative aspects, thereby unveiling the gateway to novel opportunities.

When confronted with situations that evoke frustration, endeavor to refrain from allowing negative thoughts to consume your mind. Succumbing to this pattern can result in a detrimental cycle from which extricating oneself becomes increasingly challenging.

By cultivating a curious mindset, one can stimulate cognitive processes leading to a paradigm shift, thereby experiencing a notable mitigation of frustration, irritation, and anxiety. One will become aware of the origin of each emotion.

Emotions arise as a result of a signal, regardless of the disparity in stimuli, since the signal carries the emotion. This occurrence transpires with remarkable speed, akin to a fleeting moment. The sole means to accomplish this objective is by decelerating the pace, engaging in deliberate deep breaths, and executing the cognitive process with reduced velocity.

Prior to encountering the individual in question, it is imperative to acknowledge one's own self as an unblemished entity, devoid of any challenges or flaws. Thus, it is necessary to pause and reflect before the commencement of the subsequent cycle.

To close this part, remember, find the track for emotion, destroy the signal and immediately change it with a future where you have no problems and you are curious. By carrying out this task, you will observe a significant transformation.

Strategies for mitigating or alleviating depression

Adverse emotions commonly arise in connection with auditory stimuli, specifically internalized voices. I would like to offer you some suggestions to assist you in coping with depression.

Depression can be profoundly disabling, posing considerable challenges in terms of managing its effects. It is crucial to reconsider the underlying rationale, as the phenomenon of depression appears incongruous when one internalizes an issue or unfavorable information.

Depression is a psychological condition characterized by a pervasive state of anhedonia, causing individuals to consistently lack motivation and interest in engaging in various activities, ultimately leading to the establishment of this disengaged state as a routine. Living with feelings of depression, facing adversity from the world, or harboring a sense of hopelessness can be an arduous existence. During these challenging moments, I encourage you to embark on a journey inward, exploring the depths of your being, in order to ascertain what unfolds.

Please recall that there exists no adversary within. If you are experiencing discomfort and are unsure of its cause, it is advisable to consider the possibility that there may be underlying positive factors contributing to your state. It implies the presence of an inner force striving to benefit you, even in adverse circumstances.

Take heed of your inner intuition; should it persistently echo, there are a few actions you should undertake: disengage from your present perception, effectively detaching yourself to observe from outside. Should a vocal manifestation occur, it is preferable for it to emanate from a distance within the room.

Enhance the vocal allure by imbuing it with a seductive tone reminiscent of a child's gentle yawn, possibly evoking a soothing effect conducive to inducing sleep. The concept revolves around discerning the thought processes that lead to the occurrence of certain emotions, and subsequently intervening in the sequence.

One may explore various alterations in submodalities in order to attain respite from feelings of heaviness, darkness, deep silence, or internalized burdens.

Comprehending the Fundamentals of the Neuro-Linguistic Programming Concept

The initial factor in comprehending NLP lies within the core vocabulary encompassed by the NLP concept. The fundamental principle underlying NLP posits that establishing a connection between the neural network within one's body and the linguistic expressions, encompassing both verbal and non-verbal forms, can effectively shape the behavioral patterns employed in pursuit of desired objectives.

Neurology

Neurology pertains to the functioning of the human nervous system. Prior to delving into this matter, it is imperative that we first direct our attention towards the various constituents of the nervous system, specifically focusing on the central nervous system. This encompasses the ability to engage in deliberate cognitive processes, the capacity to store and categorize information, as well as the preparation and execution of behavioral responses. Furthermore, we must also consider the peripheral nervous system, which assumes responsibility for the reflexive actions taken in response to unforeseen and immediate situations, without the need for prior cognitive processing.

The human nervous system serves as a conduit through which the body gathers sensory information from the environment and subsequently analyzes and interprets it within the realm of the mind. The apparatus employs the five fundamental sensory faculties: auditory, gustatory, kinesthetic, olfactory, and visual. By utilizing auditory perception, taste, tactile sensations, movement, olfactory senses, and vision, the cognitive faculties within will assimilate the external environment.

Now, let us proceed to examine the functioning of the central nervous system. The central nervous system (CNS) serves as the primary source of all human cognitive processes, including thought generation, decision-making, and interpretation. In any given circumstance, our central nervous system diligently evaluates its surroundings and subsequently executes actions based on one of two options, resulting in a distinct physiological response within our body.

• Drawing upon past recollections: the recollections retained within our memory can be summoned to steer the mind in its decision-making process under comparable circumstances.

• Given the external circumstances, when faced with an unfamiliar situation, the human mind evokes a deeply ingrained reaction based on our upbringing and the environment in which we have lived.

It is apparent that all aspects, ranging from memory to the world, undergo processing within the human brain and subsequently impact our cognitive processes. Consequently, individuals faced with comparable circumstances may employ disparate methodologies in addressing the issue at hand. This difference arises predominantly from the discrepancy in individuals' cognitive interpretations.

Hence, it is imperative to possess the skills to categorize and retrieve this information with utmost efficiency and effectiveness. The utilization of Natural Language Processing facilitates the exact accomplishment of such a task.

Language

Linguistics is the second parameter of the NLP. Linguistics entails the examination and analysis of language in its rudimentary or elemental manifestation. It denotes the means employed to convey our thoughts into action and articulate our perspectives. Although it may appear exaggerated, language arguably constitutes the most pivotal element in attaining a fruitful and pragmatic objective.

The language acquisition of an individual is predicated upon the assimilation and processing of sensory information. The information pertaining to the auditory sense is presented with contextualization and description, wherein it is referred to as sound.

Similarly, the sense of taste is described as taste, the kinesthetic sense as a feeling, the olfactory sense as smell, and the visual sense as images. These interpretations are subsequently expressed through both oral and non-verbal means.

A notable drawback experienced by individuals in modern times is the issue of miscommunication. They possess a deficiency in effectively expressing their viewpoints, and their attempts to do so often result in hasty speech. This also prompts a varied response from the message recipient, thereby impeding the sender's cognitive efficiency. In considering external communication, it is similarly crucial to recognize the significance of internal communication, as the human mind maintains an ongoing and unwavering dialogue within itself, influencing decision-making and comprehension of situations. Effective internal communication necessitates transparency, comprehensiveness, and dependability as well.

Programming

Once the mind and language have been optimized for optimal outcomes, it is imperative to establish a harmonious synchronization between the two elements. This synchronization involves programming the mind and developing a mastery of language to enable the mind to function at its finest capacity.

The initial phase entails arranging our thoughts, emotions, and concepts in order to enhance cognitive functionality. As the commonly quoted adage suggests, "Idleness is the breeding ground for negativity!" Awkwardness can be likened to a warehouse within the body, where unforeseen and untimely emotional eruptions can ensue, impeding the efficiency and effectiveness of both work-related and personal endeavors.

This is the process in programming where emotions are effectively managed and prevented from disrupting a specific situation in which they are unnecessary. Frequently, due to an overabundance of information, the human brain may become perplexed regarding the precise information necessary to generate in a given situation. In this instance, programming serves the purpose of systematically organizing and classifying stored information in order to enhance the efficiency of data processing.

Programming is the collective outcome of orchestrating one's sentiments, thoughts, and behaviors through assimilating sensory stimuli and rendering one's language comprehensible. Your actions will serve as a catalyst for change in the external world. For instance, the employee is situated at his workstation, encompassed by a multitude of documents that require processing and timely dispatching on the following day.

His senses are overwhelmed by a plethora of sensations, including the sound of his manager expressing a deep desire for the completion of the tasks, as well as the visual indication provided by the ticking of the clock, serving as a relentless reminder of time passing by. Subsequently, he inhales deeply and proceeds to inform his colleague that he shall be unable to meet the deadline for completing his assigned tasks. Upon the departure of all his colleagues, he rationalizes that his professional trajectory is futile and he might as well relinquish his efforts, return home, and leave the task incomplete. Upon the conclusion of his extended work period, he was unable to successfully finish his task and departed for his residence.

The underlying principle of NLP suggests that had the employee possessed a more favorable mindset and employed a different range of verbal expressions, he may have exhibited proficiency in his role. Rather than experiencing a sense of defeat, his mental condition ought to have been characterized by feelings of triumph and achievement. Rather than employing words to circumvent failure, he ought to have employed language to anticipate triumph. In the field of NLP, it is not the passage of time or the workload that elicited the decline, but rather the employee's own actions, specifically stemming from his mental state and verbal expressions.

Achievement can thus be attained not by initially altering the external world, but rather by transforming the internal world within oneself. By assuming command over the manner in which you perceive the data yielded by your sensory faculties and the manner in which you transform these interpretations into verbal expressions, you can effectively imbue yourself with the requisite or preferred courses of action. When adjustments are made to one's conduct in response to shifts within one's internal state, there will be a corresponding transformation in the external environment.

Representational Systems

Your cognitive faculty is an intricately crafted mosaic, composed of an array of distinct and remarkable sensory impressions both recalled from the past and meticulously reconstructed. All of your maps are created in this manner. We employ equivalent neural pathways for the direct, internal, and indirect apprehension of phenomena. When engaging in the process of recollection, we are actively stimulating the neural pathways and regions of the cerebral cortex that were involved in the original experience.

Essentially, this implies that we are utilizing our sensory faculties to perceive the external world. We employ the identical faculties to internally represent the encounters that we undergo.

Within the field of natural language processing, a concept known as the Preferred Representational System exists. When you have a preferred system or map of reality, it means that you gravitate toward one of the senses more than any other.

A significant portion of individuals primarily engage in visual thinking, although not all individuals employ this cognitive process. There are individuals who regard it as challenging. Some individuals may engage in self-dialogue to a greater extent than others, seeking a heightened auditory experience, whereas others may rely on their emotional response to a situation when making decisions. Individuals who possess an appreciation for the more refined tastes in existence may structure their entire lifestyles around anticipating and indulging in the upcoming extraordinary dining experiences. Certain individuals heavily depend on their olfactory faculties to caution them of potential hazards or favorable circumstances.

The predominant viewpoint among individuals is that their thought processes and emotional experiences primarily revolve around visual representations, auditory stimuli, and sensory perceptions. All individuals utilize their full range of senses, yet it is typically through the sense that feels the most refined and honed that an individual's talents and aptitudes are often revealed. Allow me to provide an illustrative instance to elucidate my point: "

Visual—Architect/Designer

Auditory—Musician/Composer

Kinesthetic—Athlete/Actor

Olfactory—Perfumer/Hunter

Gustatory—Chef/Food Critic

Every individual avails themselves of their complete array of sensory faculties, wherein our Representational System is intricately woven with our encounters in the realm of the senses. In what manner do you personally choose to perceive and engage with your own lived experience?

Reframing

The practice of employing reframing as a strategic method holds considerable potential across a wide range of situations. In this chapter, we will elucidate several methodologies aimed at altering the manner in which you appraise the occurrences you have encountered, with the objective of fostering a sense of resourcefulness and diminishing the perception of being subject to external circumstances.

Quick Example

Imagine a scenario where you are calmly engaged in your personal affairs, patiently queueing at your preferred fast-food establishment for a burger. You perceive a low and wrathful voice emanating from the rear, inherently delivering a menacing whisper into your ear:

Excuse me, it has come to my attention that your presence in this particular location is not appropriate. If you do not depart promptly, I will promptly commence actions that will greatly impede your progress."

Currently, in light of the circumstances, what are your sentiments upon contemplating this situation? Envision a scenario in which you possessed the ability to perceive the speaker to be a full 12 inches taller than your own height. How do you feel? The level of significance you attribute to the event is closely associated with the emotions you experience. The events in question embody nothing but pure, unadulterated data. The manner in which we interpret those occurrences, often at a subconscious level and with rapidity, is what elicits our response, rather than the occurrences themselves. If we were to imagine that you were unaware of the fact that this scenario serves as an illustration on how to reframe situations, and instead believe it to be unfolding in real-time, what emotions would you experience? The majority of individuals would likely experience a strong inclination toward defensiveness. Violated. Scared. Imagine if you were able to reorient yourself and happened to encounter an exceedingly furious countenance. Subsequently, within a brief span of seconds, the countenance of anger underwent a transformation into one of embarrassment.

I deeply apologize for my mistake, as I had mistakenly believed you to be my neighbor. He made a commitment to his spouse that he would cease consuming fast food. This individual experienced a cardiac event a few months ago, and it is now disconcerting to find oneself in this situation."

What is your current emotional state? Relieved? How do you anticipate your subsequent emotional state when reflecting upon the occurrence or recounting the experience to acquaintances after a few days? It is highly likely that recounting this incident would result in an amusing anecdote that would evoke laughter merely through contemplation.

Excessive Dependence on the Environment for Significance

The fact remains that in the absence of physical contact, the laws of physics, chemistry, and biology dictate the manner in which events should be interpreted, leaving no prescribed guidelines. Furthermore, it is imperative to grasp that reframing personal events entails a distinct process rather than a single, one-time application of a commonly taught NLP tactic. However, it is quite straightforward. This is applicable to any past occurrence that elicits a sensation of diminished resourcefulness whenever it is recollected.

Daily Events

Suppose an individual abruptly changes lanes in front of you while driving. You get angry. Most of us feel violated in some way. It appears that they did not deem us significant enough to extend the courtesy of a signal. We experience a sense of objectification, leading to an emotional response characterized by anger. However, in the event that you were intentionally to alter the course of that occurrence, thereby providing them with a motive to refrain from giving a signal, what would be the resulting outcome? Perhaps they have recently been terminated from their employment. Perhaps the presentation of utmost importance has slipped their mind, and it is now a mere five minutes away. It is possible that they received news indicating that their child was involved in a motor vehicle accident. Perhaps they are believed to be under the influence of a wrathful spirit. It is probable that the individual is currently experiencing a bee sting in the genital area.

Difficult Process

The most challenging aspect of this process is the inherent satisfaction derived from assuming the role of a victim. To a certain extent, there exists a collective inclination among individuals to assume the role of a victim, thereby attributing the blame of their predicaments to external factors, rather than embracing personal accountability in order to address and resolve their own challenges. A significant number of individuals yearn for retribution against those who have inflicted harm upon them. Numerous politicians secure their election based precisely on this commitment:

The issues you are experiencing are not attributable to any fault on your part. They bear responsibility for someone else's actions. If you elect me, I will take appropriate disciplinary actions against those individuals."

They do not explicitly express this, but that is typically the essence of their message. Furthermore, it is frequently the case that they are indeed responsible for the unfavourable outcome. However, in accordance with the proverbial wisdom, should one pursue vengeance, it is imperative to prepare two burial plots. Indeed, while it may be tempting to seek retribution, (or at least entertain the notion) it ultimately proves to be ineffective. If one does not adhere to the ancient Chinese principle of eliminating not only one's adversary, but also their associates, relatives, and acquaintances to thwart any potential retaliation, it is inevitable that there will be individuals who seek retribution for the vengeful actions enacted upon them. Notwithstanding the portrayal of revenge in numerous Hollywood films, it remains evident that this vengeful pursuit lacks efficacy as a personal strategy for attaining success. No individual achieved wealth, developed romantic relationships, or left a lasting influence on society by seeking vengeance upon their adversaries. They did so by out-framing and forgetting their enemies. To be sure, if you do have any true enemies, or people that wish you ill will, you need to protect yourself. But for people who cut you off in traffic, or break up with you without the decency of telling you, or backstabbing coworkers, it's best to just ignore them and get on with life. This procedure will assist you in accomplishing that.

Step One

The initial stage involves documenting the distressing incident in a manner that is as impartial and factual as feasible. An individual rudely maneuvered ahead of me without utilizing their turn signal. My romantic partner has ceased communication with me, eliminated my access to her on the social media platform Facebook, and has not responded to any messages or phone calls in a span of three months. On each occasion when I enter the break room within my workplace, individuals abruptly cease their conversations and direct their gaze towards me.

Step Two

Devise a purpose attributed to their motivation that both clarifies their behavior and evokes positive emotions within you. Those are the sole regulations. Subsequently, proceed with composing the event by incorporating those intentions into its framework.

An individual was operating a vehicle when an insect inadvertently entered his ocular region, followed by a venomous reptile inflicting a bite on his reproductive organ, causing an erratic change in his driving trajectory that brought him into my path. I am grateful that I am not in his position.

My significant other attended a social gathering where a Satanic ritual took place, during which she consumed a mysterious concoction and made a pledge to conceive and bear a child for Satan. I am grateful that I am no longer in a relationship with her.

Due to unidentified factors, individuals in the workplace hold the perception of me as a sorcerer. They hold the belief that uttering an incorrect statement in my presence would result in a drastic impairment of their cognitive faculties, akin to the transformation of their cerebral matter into a viscous consistency akin to that of pancake batter.

The sole regulations pertain to imbuing their conduct with an alternative intent, which evokes a sense of upliftment upon contemplation, rather than a sense of dismay. And by using the term "better," we are exclusively referring to a highly adaptive emotional response such as inwardly expressing amusement.

Experiment

To commence, it might require a certain level of creativity. This entails an alternative method that does not involve a singular peculiar technique capable of instantaneously transforming the world around you into a perpetual celebration of love. This is a skill. With increased practice of this skill, your proficiency in it will improve. The ultimate objective of this initiative is to abstain from making any presumptions about the behaviors of others. Even when you possess an understanding of the underlying motives, construct alternative rationales for those motives. Unless you're being stalked by an ax murder, with a little creativity you can at least find a reason to pity and laugh at your enemies. It is possible that during their childhood, they were confined to a basement and sustained solely with a regimen of canine sustenance. The sole objective is to derive enhanced emotional well-being when contemplating past events, rather than experiencing any deterioration in mood.

Deeper Intentions

By engaging in the practice of transforming the recounting of an event, whether recent or from the past, on a daily basis, you will gradually modify your manner of referencing occurrences. Over time, you will effectively eliminate any distressing recollections from your past, reshaping them into memories devoid of discomfort. This, in its essence, will imbue you with a significant degree of personal autonomy and influence. However, at a more profound level, you will be cultivating the ability to perceive reality as significantly more adaptable than its inherent nature suggests. You will experience a heightened sense of autonomy, regardless of the absence of direct control over the circumstances. It is one matter to cite renowned individuals who articulate clever phrases like, 'The impact stems not from occurrences, but from the significance we assign to them,' but it is an entirely different matter to personally experience this truth on a profound level. This process will require a considerable amount of time, but once you reach that critical moment, your perspective will become forward-looking, with the conviction that regardless of any circumstances, as long as there is no tangible interaction, I possess the ability to attribute any desired meaning to it."

NLP Simplified

How Does NLP Work?

NLP offers individuals an avenue to exert influence on their subconscious mind with the aim of modifying their responses to external stimuli.

Did you reach a juncture in your life wherein you made a deliberate decision to amend a particular behavior that you found displeasing, subsequently experimenting with alternative approaches, only to inadvertently revert back to the original habit? What are your thoughts on the reasons behind your repetition of the same behavior, despite your efforts to modify it?

The latent power of your subconscious mind surpasses that of your conscious mind. Unconscious repositories house negative emotions, limiting behaviors, and undesired beliefs. In order to modify them, this is the destination we must proceed to. NLP has the potential to assist you in achieving this!

Similar to how chain-smokers cannot abruptly quit smoking and alcoholics cannot easily cease drinking, our limiting beliefs possess the same level of difficulty to overcome. It is conceivable that you are permitting an ideology that originated during your youth to engender a diminished sense of self-worth, or alternatively, this constraining belief may be impeding your utmost capabilities within a particular facet of your life or profession. One illustration would be the belief that one is devoid of any affection from others. This is merely a conjecture; it does not necessarily imply its veracity. One could alter their belief system and consequently enhance their sense of self-worth.

Frequently, individuals exhibit behavior without conscious intent, rather than through deliberate consciousness. NLP facilitates the recognition and understanding of unproductive reactions and behaviors, enabling their substitution with more favorable alternatives that empower individuals to lead a maximized existence.

Two NLP Fundamental Assumptions

The human perception of reality is intricately shaped by the cognitive processes of the brain. It is a reflection of individuals' sensory experiences and environmental influences, rather than an absolute understanding of the objective nature of the world. NLP is a modality that facilitates the cognitive restructuring of one's neural pathways at the subconscious level in order to attain a specific intended result.

Life and mind can be conceptualized as systematic phenomena - The human body, societal structures, and the fabric of the universe collectively constitute a complex network of interdependent systems and subsystems, mutually influencing one another in profound ways. These systems originate from a particular self-organizational philosophy and inherently strive for the attainment of optimal states of equilibrium.

NLP is currently being employed for the purpose of crafting business strategies and enhancing leadership capabilities. It also offers tools to the world of business to boost the health, efficiency, and communication skills of individuals who work together.

One can employ NLP techniques and perceptions as a means to enhance cognitive control, regulate emotions, and govern behavior. This practice facilitates self-management and enables effective interpersonal connections.

Natural Language Processing (NLP) comprises a dynamic compendium of knowledge coupled with a futuristic perspective on human existence, supported by a diverse repertoire of techniques aimed at enhancing cognitive, emotional, and behavioral faculties.

Acquiring knowledge in Natural Language Processing (NLP) will afford you the opportunity to:

• Strive to improve upon tasks that you already perform with sound judgement and efficiency, or aim to exceed your current level of proficiency.

• Acquire the necessary skills and perspectives to effectively engage in tasks that may not be immediately within your capabilities, but are of interest to you.

- Think more clearly.

- Converse more efficiently with people.

- Assume command over your thoughts, moods, and behaviors. • Exercise authority over your thoughts, moods, and behaviors. • Establish mastery over your thoughts, moods, and behaviors.

Taking into account all relevant factors, the most concise explanation of the concept of NLP can be phrased as follows: NLP serves as a practical guidebook for unlocking the potential of the human mind, enabling individuals to effectively utilize the mental language in order to consistently attain predetermined and desirable results.

Common Misconceptions About NLP

Misconception #1: NLP is mind control and manipulative

Instances of individuals being manipulated by others through the use of neuro-linguistic programming (NLP) are nonexistent, yet employing NLP techniques can indeed exert influence over others. Frequently, individuals encounter difficulty when it comes to exerting self-control. NLP facilitates the establishment of more profound rapport with individuals and enables one to exert influence, given that we possess the ability to regulate our own emotions. This does not involve the manipulation of another person's thoughts or behaviors. It's controlling our own.

Misconception #2: NLP doesn't or will not work for me

It is not always the case that individuals achieve immediate success in their endeavors with NLP. An indispensable competency in the field of NLP lies in the aptitude to adapt and modify one's behaviors and actions accordingly. This phenomenon is referred to as "behavioral adaptability." It signifies the need to attentively observe, ascertain, and attentively listen to discern indicators of the circumstances or emotional state pertaining either to oneself or the individual one seeks to establish a connection with or exert an impact upon. It is conceivable that you may already be experiencing favorable outcomes in various facets of your life. You are employing methods and strategies that may be functioning effectively for you, even without your conscious awareness. NLP possesses the capability to facilitate the identification of effective strategies and provide insights on how to further enhance their efficacy. This will assist you in making incremental adjustments as you enhance your proficiency with techniques.

Misconception #3: NLP encompasses therapeutic practices.

NLP was originally employed within the realm of therapeutic practice. However, many of the aptitudes, conduct, and strategies demonstrated significant advantages in various aspects of human conduct, specifically in relation to communication, transformation, and persuasion. Presently, natural language processing (NLP) finds application in various domains such as sports, leadership, sales, coaching, and public speaking. Occasionally, individuals are able to overcome their negative habits or transcend their limited beliefs in a single sitting. So NLP is more than therapy. It bestows therapeutic advantages for a multitude of activities such as restful slumber, rejuvenating getaways, melodic appreciation, literary indulgence, communing with nature, and engaging in mindful contemplation.

In the domain of healthcare

NLP is highly suitable for physicians, nursing personnel, and other individuals within the healthcare sector, given the rapid evolution of healthcare delivery. It is apparent that the demand extends beyond mere medical and nursing expertise. There is a growing expectation among patients within the contemporary healthcare system for the personnel employed therein to possess exceptional levels of social competence and adaptability.

This encompasses the ability to negotiate effectively, a proactive attitude towards conflict resolution, and a requisite level of proficiency in business management. This notion stems from the belief that the process of healing is intricately associated with both the deeply held beliefs and effective communication practiced with patients. The social environment and physical layout of medical facilities and clinics exert an equally enduring influence on the recuperative journey.

Neuro-linguistic programming offers strategies for enabling medical professionals to establish collaborative and harmonious connections with both their colleagues and patients, facilitating effective, concise, and unambiguous communication that supports the promotion of health. In recent times, there has been a growing emphasis on neuro-linguistic programming, wherein NLP increasingly incorporates facets pertaining to the adaptation and preservation of personal well-being, the mitigation of stress, the activation of the body's inherent self-healing capabilities, and the exploration of methods to comprehend the intricate interplay between manifested assumptions, attitudes, beliefs, and one's state of health.

The foundation of this inquiry lies in the following query: "What delineates individuals who successfully recuperate from an ailment, as opposed to those who fail to prevail over their illness?" This area of investigation undergoes continual development.

Creativity

Artistic individuals, including authors, writers, songwriters, musicians, and singers, who have partaken in NLP training or coaching, hold the conviction that they have acquired significant knowledge and profound perspectives from their experiences. They have come to perceive the impediments to a creative mindset and have gained insight into fostering it. Hence, the aforementioned approach known as the Disney strategy emerged through the efforts of Robert Dilts in the United States. This strategy exhibits robust facets regarding the alleviation of obstacles and the rekindling of creativity.

Instruction and training

NLP additionally seeks to purposefully cultivate a comprehension of a person's cognitive acquisition and assimilation of novel knowledge within their pre-existing knowledge framework. This results in interesting strategies for teachers, trainers, and parents to gain methodical and specific access to students and to support them in achieving better performance.

Consequently, teaching methodology and leadership embody the fundamental principles of neurolinguistic programming. NLP serves as a valuable enhancement in the professional endeavors of pastors, priests, counselors, educators, and pedagogues involved in group settings.

Parental education

NLP facilitates the constructive enhancement of communication between parents and children. Through effective communication, you provide the child with the opportunity to comprehend your message and respond in an appropriate manner. If you instruct your child against engaging in a certain behavior, the likelihood of their acting contrary to your instructions will undoubtedly escalate. If the message is pronounced with a commanding tone or threatening tone of voice, the child will become frightened. An exemplary instance involves a communication wherein the expression "Do not be concerned!" induces heightened anxiety in the child. However, if you were to emphasize the importance of caution or reassure him that all is well, you would successfully accomplish your objective.

By conducting diligent observation and attentive listening, you will acquire a profound understanding of your child's manner of adapting and navigating their surroundings and their broader reality. In order to empower your child within the school environment and navigate the educational system effectively, it is essential that you demonstrate to him the process of visualizing his own circumstances. By adopting this approach, you will acquire the necessary skills to independently manage your child's condition, even if it has not yet reached the desired state. Parents are only human!

Parents who actively engage in the practice of neuro-linguistic programming provide their children with a valuable means of achieving effective, articulate communication, while equipping them with the necessary resources for fostering their

learning and cultivating a positive sense of self-worth.

Eliminating Sources of Negativity

Fear is a psychological condition that arises when an individual's mind perceives a certain stimulus as potentially harmful, leading to a subsequent alteration in cognitive processing. Various behaviors manifest when an individual experiences fear.

Firstly, residing in a state of fear impairs one's capacity to consistently make rational decisions. When you are not making rational decisions, you are not going to reach your full potential and you may end up ruining relationships, for example, because of things like you are scared to go outside and meet with your friends. Over a prolonged period of engaging in such behavior, it is conceivable that you may inadvertently alienate individuals across various spheres of your life and eventually come to the sobering realization of your solitude, stemming from a reluctance to address certain challenges that have arisen.

Our current societal landscape is characterized by a prevailing sense of fear. Simply activate the television and observe the presence of individuals engaging in reporting pertaining to distressing news narratives and assorted dreadful occurrences, which will inevitably evoke fear within you. It is imperative to acknowledge that news stations engage in such practices with the primary objective of bolstering their viewership figures. They employ such strategies as selectively covering negative occurrences in order to more effectively capture your interest in their content. The greater level of involvement with adverse content leads to increased viewership, thus contributing to a rise in the show's ratings.

Please cease watching the news. While there may be pertinent or desirable information presented, it is unnecessary to have it constantly on. If you have inquiries regarding certain information, such as the forecast for the following day, I recommend referring to the official website of the news station to find the pertinent weather details.

Given the prevailing apprehension within our society, it is often overlooked that we possess the capacity to seize control over our lives and undertake the endeavor of cultivating a mindset detached from fear and negativity. Our subconscious mind is inclined to perceive and amplify the fear and negativity present in our surroundings.

Make a deliberate endeavor to eradicate sources of negativity from your life. For instance, if you consistently engage in the consumption of news content and experience a sense of despondency due to the prevalence of negative occurrences, endeavor to consciously reduce your exposure to such content and assess its impact on your emotional well-being.

Distance yourself from individuals who consistently seek out financial vulnerabilities. It might prove challenging, as the individuals in question can, at times, be members of your own family. However, it is not imperative for you to consistently subject yourself to their presence. One can adopt measures to restrict the amount of time spent with such individuals in order to actively work towards avoiding their negative impact.

Please identify two sources of negativity within your life and formulate a commitment to reduce their impact over the course of the upcoming week. Taking the news as an example, this could imply dedicating only a limited amount of time towards acquainting oneself with current events at the close of the day, rather than spending several hours watching news broadcasts. The objective is not to be oblivious to current events or to live in seclusion, but rather to consciously recognize the emotional impact of the content we select to engage with.

Having successfully identified the two sources of negativity and committed to mitigating their impact over the upcoming week, it is now imperative to record your observations regarding the effects of minimizing these influences on your emotional well-being. Have you exhibited a greater sense of optimism? Enhanced consciousness regarding the subconscious impact of everyday stimuli?

Our conscious mind effectively imparts instructions to our subconscious mind, which dutifully follows without raising any inquiries or objections. The information received is considered as fact, prompting appropriate actions to be taken in order to realize the desired objective envisioned by the conscious mind.

Therefore, it is imperative to recognize that in assessing your life, the independent operation of your subconscious mind is insufficient; rather, it necessitates clear guidance to ensure the manifestation of intentional measures. However, this phenomenon presents a challenge for the mind in distinguishing between reality and illusion. A highly effective approach to maintaining a grounded state is by ensuring that you are constantly immersed in a positive ambiance. If one consistently immerses oneself in an environment characterized by negativity, it becomes increasingly arduous to discern the veracity of matters.

An instance of this can be observed when you are actively engaging in the consumption of news media and come across an unfortunate event occurring within your immediate community. In order to ensure personal safety, it is recommended to install a comprehensive security system, thereby ensuring round-the-clock protection, even during periods of rest. However, in the event of hearing a disturbance during nocturnal hours, discerning its authenticity becomes challenging due to the influence of this trepidation. One might naturally infer that upon perceiving a potential intrusion into one's dwelling, an individual would instinctively undertake the necessary measures in response, anchored in their perception of reality as the impetus behind their ensuing actions.

If we succumb to fear, we risk perceiving the world through a lens of negativity, thus inducing self-inflicted limitations. When engaging in such actions, it appears that the global community becomes predisposed towards targeting and reproaching you. One's perspective determines their perception of the world, and although it may initially be narrow, over time it becomes ingrained.

The manner in which one perceives the world will determine their lived experiences. If one has a propensity to view the world through a negative lens, it will inevitably taint their perception of every encountered experience as unfavorable. It is possible to experience a positive event and subsequently find oneself anticipating the occurrence of a negative event. Therefore, rather than seeking the positive aspect, you are directing your attention towards the aperture in your pocket through which your coins continue to elude you.

For instance, in the scenario where you acquire a new employment opportunity and commence the training process, it is conceivable that if you do not grasp the material as quickly as you perceive you should, you may soon find yourself viewing this experience not as an opportunity for personal growth and acquisition of new knowledge, but rather as an anticipation of the moment when your supervisor summons you to their office and terminates your employment. This unfortunate situation arises solely from your pessimistic outlook on the world.

You exert agency over the course of your existence, indeed! Echoing the wisdom of Alice Walker, "The relinquishment of one's power often stems from the mistaken belief of its absence." Despite the pervasive negativity in your surroundings, it is not obligatory for you to adopt a similar disposition. To eliminate or at least minimize the influence of negativity, thus enabling you to liberate yourself from a perpetual state of fear and negativity, you can proactively undertake measures to enhance the quality of your life.

Ultimately, the experience of depression engenders a sense of helplessness, yet resolution will not be achieved autonomously. The pervasive negativity permeating the world will exacerbate your depression due to the overwhelming sense of fear you will experience. Regardless of your efforts, it is impossible to shield oneself completely from all potential threats. Consequently, a sense of powerlessness may arise when attempting to ensure the safety of yourself and your loved ones, ultimately leading to feelings of despondency due to an inability to guarantee their protection. It entails an unceasing predicament from which one inevitably becomes entangled, and the sole means of extricating oneself is by relinquishing pessimistic perspectives and adopting a truthful perception of reality.

You need not view the world through an excessively optimistic lens, but it is also unnecessary to constantly seek out flaws and shortcomings in every situation. Discover the middle ground and acknowledge that you have the capacity to exert influence over your own life, yet accept that there are limitations to the extent of control one can have over life's circumstances. Events are bound to occur and circumstances may arise beyond one's control, rendering any preventative measures futile.

Assumption 2: The identity of individuals should not be equated with their behavioral actions.

The meaning:

Your behavior is in no way reflective of your personal character. The appropriateness or inappropriateness of your behavior is not contingent upon your ethical principles.

The recommended course of action:

It is imperative that you take the necessary steps to modify your behavior, while simultaneously embracing your current state. Assess your actions critically and make appropriate adjustments, if deemed necessary.

It is imperative to adopt an accepting approach towards individuals. I understand that there may be instances where you perceive some individuals as morally questionable, but it is not within our purview to pass judgment upon them. Regard them simply as individuals with inherent human qualities.

One can choose to reject their behavior, provide guidance for improvement, but refrain from making judgments about their inherent nature.

The advantages that you will receive:

It is apparent that altering one's behavior, or rather our habits, is necessary in order to bring about a transformative change in one's life. NLP endeavors to assist individuals in comprehending and enhancing their awareness of the malleability of their habits and counterproductive behaviors, emphasizing that such patterns are not fixed, but rather decisions that can be altered at any given juncture.

In this presupposition, limited elaboration was provided as a result of its close resemblance to the subsequent presupposition. In the forthcoming chapter, a comprehensive explication will be offered, enabling comprehension of both this presupposition and the following one.

Presumption 3: Individuals lack malicious intentions.

"Even in the face of adversity, I maintain my belief in the inherent goodness of humanity." - Anne Frank

The meaning:

If I were to inform you that the entire human population throughout history does not harbor malevolent intentions, I anticipate your response would be: "Nevertheless, what about the individuals who engage in acts of murder, assault, and sexual violence?"

Alright, could you recall the preceding presupposition in question? Individuals should be regarded separately from their behavior, implying that one's actions do not necessarily reflect their intentions being malicious. For a more comprehensive understanding, consider the following illustration.

I would appreciate it if you could recollect a past incident in which you engaged in behavior that was considered inappropriate. Do you believe that your actions were motivated by a lack of moral character? Probably not. Numerous individuals tend to evaluate others based on their conduct, deeming those who engage in virtuous actions as inherently good individuals, whereas those who partake in negative behaviors as inherently bad individuals; however, this oversimplified judgment should not be considered appropriate or accurate. Given that human behavior is unaffected by external factors.

On certain occasions, individuals may find themselves subject to such strong feelings of anger that they unintentionally utter offensive language, even if their typical demeanor is characterized by politeness. In light of this observation, it begs the question: does the utterance of such language amidst an outburst of anger imply a fundamental deficiency in one's sense of politeness? Of course not. However, were someone to evaluate you based on your conduct, they would likely conclude that you exhibit a lack of respect and courtesy.

Simply observe the thief as he commits the act of theft. Do you believe that his actions were motivated by intrinsic moral deficiency? Alternatively, it could be due to his intention to solely provide sustenance for himself. Certainly, he displayed inappropriate conduct; however, it does not necessarily imply that he possesses inherently negative character traits.

There is a significant number of individuals who exhibit a propensity for passing critical judgments and engaging in gossip about others. However, when inquired about their own evaluation, individuals tend to assert their virtuous behavior. I am aware that there exists a considerable number of individuals who proclaim themselves as innocent and virtuous despite having engaged in wrongdoing in the past. If one were to inquire about their actions, one might pose the question, how could they have perpetrated such acts? Their response is influenced by the "wyz" circumstance, or due to his need to... This is the crux of the matter — while his actions were inappropriate, his intentions were not malevolent.

Consider this perspective: When examining individuals who have engaged in negative behavior, it begs the question whether they truly possess innate maliciousness or if their actions stem from unfulfilled aspects within their lives.

While I do not condone negative behavior, a careful examination of the underlying causes may reveal that individuals harbored positive intentions within them.

The course of action that you are expected to undertake:

Abstain from passing judgment upon individuals observing them engage in wrongful behavior, for one cannot ascertain the inner complexities of their being. Engaging in the practice of making judgments about others can lead to the adoption of a negative perspective and may also result in disdain from others. Alternatively, assess your own actions, with a focus on initiating personal growth and rectifying any detrimental behaviors or habits.

It is imperative to consistently seek understanding of individuals and actively engage in listening, as the acquisition of proficient listening and communication skills is of utmost significance. By doing so, one is likely to gain the respect of others. In the event that someone seeks your assistance or counsel, it is essential to refrain from passing judgment in the event that they divulge information concerning their past.

When observing an individual engaging in undesirable conduct and desiring to offer guidance, it is advisable to direct attention towards their intentions rather than the reasons behind their actions. For instance, when offering counsel to dissuade someone from engaging in the wrongful act of taking belongings that do not belong to them, it is important to abstain from passing judgment and labeling them as a thief. Instead, direct attention towards comprehending the underlying motivation behind their actions which may be rooted in a positive intention. It will become evident to you that his unfavorable conduct was spurred by his financial need (well-intentioned). Therefore, it would be prudent of you to offer him counsel on viable means of securing an income, such as undertaking employment or initiating a business venture.

"The advantages that you will receive: "The positive outcomes that you will obtain: "The perks that will be bestowed upon you:

Once you come to recognize the purity of your intentions, you will become aware that what is required is a modification of your conduct or patterns. You will be contributing to assisting individuals in making transformative changes to their daily routines, thereby enabling their professional growth and development as either a coach or mentor.

Additionally, adopting a positive outlook towards others is crucial. It is important to remain composed and understand that individuals may exhibit negative behavior as a result of lacking something significant in their lives, leading them to seek fulfillment through inappropriate means. Thus, you will acquire the ability to proffer accurate counsel.

The optimal course of action, should you maintain a steadfast belief in the inherent goodness of others, is to adopt the role of a person who grants forgiveness. By doing so, you will possess a deeper understanding of the fact that the individual who has caused you harm did not possess ill-intentions.

Transform states without resources into states with resources.

Resource states have the capability to encompass any contemporary instance in which an individual faces insufficient resources.

Allow me to present a straightforward illustration: amidst the autumnal chill and moisture permeating the streets, the entire expanse of the sky is obscured by clouds, depriving the world of sunlight for an extended period. Having been subjected to rainfall, you find yourself contemplating measures to prevent the onset of a cold. Please draw upon an appropriate reservoir of personal experiences. For instance, recollect the peaceful respite by the seaside, basking under the radiant sun while the world bathed in its luminosity, evoking a sense of an inner radiance.

Illuminate the radiance within yourself, and your circumstances shall undergo a transformation. You shall find solace in the warmth, and even amid the rain, the essence of spring shall engulf your surroundings.

A compilation of resource states can prove advantageous in intricate circumstances, such as instances where one lacks self-assurance.

Frequently, there arise situations where we are required to carry out tasks in unfamiliar environments, where our self-assurance may be lacking. Indeed, every nascent enterprise typically commences in a state of precariousness. If we perpetually limited ourselves to pursuing only tasks of which we possessed absolute certainty, we would forever remain oblivious to new knowledge and forego any opportunity for advancement.

Therefore, insecurity is not a reason to refuse something. The regulation "In cases of uncertainty, it is preferable to refrain from overtaking" is advisable while driving. A frequently encountered piece of advice in life is to proceed despite uncertainty, with the statement: "Not sure - do it!"

Indeed, however, it would be prudent to commence the task by initially procuring the required resources for your own use. Subsequently, one may proceed to undertake the task from the resource state, irrespective of any uncertainties.

If one lacks knowledge and direction, where can they access these resources? It is rather straightforward: you may retrieve them once more from the container, provided that you possess sufficient expertise in the matter. Although the skills may not hold practical value for you, you can still derive intrinsic benefits, such as self-assurance, a sense of control, and mastery, from the experience itself.

Let us consider another instance where it becomes necessary to compose an article. Assuming you have no prior experience in article writing and lack the knowledge to proceed with this task.

You are currently situated in a state lacking sufficient resources, wherein the likelihood of achieving a successful outcome is deemed to be low.

What course of action should be pursued in this particular situation? Reflect upon your areas of competence, those in which you possess familiarity and proficiency, where you feel at ease and effortlessly skilled. As an illustration, you may lack proficiency in written composition, yet possess exceptional oral communication skills. Please bear in mind the role of a narrator as you engage in storytelling. Immerse yourself in this state and embrace the act of writing. Craft your words as though you are openly expressing yourself, at ease in your thoughts. And you will undoubtedly achieve success.

If you possess proficient writing skills yet struggle with public speaking and find yourself in need of delivering a speech, the converse holds true: recall the mental state you assume when writing and apply it to your speaking endeavors!

One could potentially associate a resource state with an action that appears to have no discernible connection to it. For instance, should you be required to deliver a presentation, you possess doubts about your ability to manage the task at hand. However, simultaneously you exhibit flawless swimming skills. Ensure that your report remains completely unrelated to swimming. Proceed to the lectern, platform, or seat in the same state in which you enter the water. Do bear in mind your physical state as you execute decisive and forceful actions to traverse the expanse of water. Experience a sense of self-assurance in your swimming abilities, even when faced with unfamiliar circumstances, in order to enhance your ability to navigate challenging tasks.

It is absolutely not necessary to actually imagine yourself in the water and remember all the sensations associated with swimming. Keep in mind solely the state of self-assurance, composed authority, mastery over your physical being, dominion over the circumstances, the stance of the superior, the outlook of capability, the mindset of triumph.

How Neuro-Linguistic Programming Works?

Exhibiting, engagement, and persuasive transparency are essential elements of neuro-linguistic programming. The belief is that if one observes another person successfully completing a task, the process can be replicated and shared with others, enabling them to achieve the same objective.

Advocates of neuro-linguistic programming assert that each individual should possess a personal framework to navigate and comprehend the reality that surrounds them. The practitioners of N.L.P. undertake a comprehensive analysis of their own perspectives as well as alternative viewpoints in order to construct a cohesive representation of a particular scenario. The N.L.P. client acquires information by comprehending the range of perspectives. Advocates of this line of reasoning acknowledge the indispensability of cognitive abilities in processing readily available information, as well as recognize the reciprocal influence between the physical and mental realms. Neuro-linguistic programming can be characterized as an empirical approach. Following that, should an individual desire to grasp a particular undertaking, it is imperative for them to carry out said task in order to acquire knowledge through practical experience.

N.L.P. practitioners acknowledge the presence of distinct hierarchies of acquisition, communication, and transformation. The six sequential levels of advancement are as follows:

Rationality and transcendence: This can be encompassed within a broader paradigm, such as spirituality, ethics, or an alternative conceptual framework. This represents the highest degree of advancement.

Personality: Identity refers to the essence of an individual, encompassing their responsibilities and roles undertaken in various aspects of life.

Convictions and attributes constitute your framework of convictions and the matters of significance to you.

Abilities and capabilities: These encompass your innate or acquired skills and aptitudes.

Practices: Behaviors encompass the specific actions that one engages in.

Status: Your status refers to your distinct situation or environment, encompassing additional individuals in your vicinity. This can be regarded as the utmost level of minimal progress.

The purpose of establishing and organizing each consistent level is to effectively arrange and synchronize the underlying data. As a result, implementing a modification at a lower hierarchy can potentially lead to alterations at a higher level. Regardless, the implementation of an increment at a higher level will also yield modifications at the lower levels, as posited by the N.L.P. theory.

Chapter 2: Comprehending Cognitive Processes

Are you familiar with the adage, "One's thoughts shape their identity"? Engaging in negative self-perception can contribute to a self-deprecating cycle of fulfillment. By consistently affirming that you possess qualities of indolence and insignificance, you inadvertently foster a set of behaviors that align with your perceived lack of worth or diligence. One begins to perceive oneself as the most unfavorable iteration of one's own character. This is an issue that requires concerted efforts to combat. Positive mindset significantly contributes to one's holistic well-being. Adopting an optimistic mindset will enhance your emotional well-being, cognitive focus, and overall physiological well-being.

Positive thinking involves shifting one's mindset away from negativity and embracing the appreciation of the frequent moments of beauty that we encounter. It is not that there is a lack of beauty in our lives, but rather a failure to recognize and fully embrace the abundant experiences that lie before us. Positive thinking involves changing one's perspective from a negative sentiment, such as "it is gloomy outside today and I have no desire to go to work," to a more constructive mindset, like "despite the gloomy weather, I will exert effort at work and perhaps rest later." It is important to acknowledge that positive thinking does not solely revolve around optimistic outlooks. The positive aspect must be pragmatic and achievable.

One's level of self-assurance will be significantly enhanced by embracing a mindset of positivity. Confidence is a quality that poses challenges when it comes to quantifying and nurturing. It originates from the depths of one's innermost being, and it acknowledges that individuals can ensure their own safety and well-being through their own volition. Confidence comes from self-security. If one harbors a multitude of shameful elements, such as past occurrences or other causes of humiliation, one will encounter difficulty in cultivating self-assurance. In order to possess confidence, it is imperative to relinquish all unnecessary baggage and acknowledge within oneself that they are an individual deserving of attention, receptiveness, and comprehension. Consequently, one must effectively and authentically convey their thoughts and emotions in this manner.

The most effective and enduring approach to cultivating confidence is to embrace your true self and exhibit unwavering ownership of your identity. If you possess a significant stature, embrace your height and proudly showcase it to the world. Embrace and embrace your stature if you are of lesser height. There exists a diverse range of physical attributes and a multitude of individuals who hold an affinity for individuals possessing characteristics akin to yours. Regardless of any mental or physical qualities that may give rise to insecurities, it is imperative to relinquish such anxieties and release them. This will be advantageous for your long-term development. Addressing motivation is of utmost significance in individuals who suffer from depression. Motivation plays a crucial role in the manifestation of depression. The absence of motivation is the underlying cause of depression, frequently leading to a recurrent cycle of diminished motivation and negative emotions. Motivation is an elusive notion, yet it is reasonably conclusive to state that enhanced physical well-being generally correlates with heightened levels of motivation. By devoting all of your time to addiction or indulging in unhealthy habits, you inadvertently reinforce this cycle, thereby diminishing your motivation. Regrettably, this is not an uncommon occurrence.

A significant aspect of cultivating a positive mindset involves acquiring the skill of engaging in positive self-dialogue while effectively disassociating oneself from negative thoughts. One may simply acknowledge that thoughts do not correspond to reality. There is no obligation to refute or invalidate thoughts; one can simply acknowledge their unfavorable or unnecessary nature and dismiss them. Many individuals place an excessive amount of importance on their thoughts, even the insignificant ones, as well as their content. They dedicate all of their time to strategically contemplating in order to attain a sense of fulfillment. However, contentment remains elusive.

It would be beneficial in this particular scenario to acquire the skill of self-affirmations. One is not defined by one's thoughts. The content of your mind is limited solely to your own consciousness. Occasionally, they are accurate or valid, while at other times, they are erroneous. It doesn't matter. In either scenario, they do not constitute your identity. One's moral character or judgment should not be categorically determined by their thoughts or opinions.

The Role of the Subconscious Mind in the Field of Psychology

What is the intended definition of the conscious mind? It comprises the cognitive and affective faculties that currently engage in the processes of thought, emotion, and self-expression. It serves as the deliberate origin of readily available information. The uppermost portion of the iceberg represents merely a fraction of its overall mass, whereas if one were to descend further, it becomes apparent that the majority of the iceberg lies submerged beneath the surface.

The subconscious mind consists of the collective recollections, associations, and interpersonal encounters one has amassed over time.

The subconscious mind plays a pivotal role in regulating our inherent sexual desires. It is dictated by the principle of hedonism, which fundamentally posits that we are propelled by the pursuit of pleasure and that pleasure serves as the paramount impetus. This is the reason why advertising proves to be highly effective when it incorporates concepts pertaining to sexual incentive and various other sources of enjoyment. The longstanding adage that "sex sells" remains remarkably pertinent in contemporary times. Contemplate the occurrence of sexual attraction. While one may possess a clear awareness of their marital status, experiencing contentment within it, one may still find themselves desiring to partake in intimate activities with individuals other than their partner, despite having mutually agreed upon fidelity. This encapsulates the fundamental nature of the id. It perpetually exists, discreetly awaiting, and is the utmost instinctual force. Indeed, sexuality frequently constitutes an integral component of Dark Persuasion tactics. A leader frequently exhibits an appealing physical presence. This phenomenon is indicative of charisma and exhibits a highly efficacious method of appealing to an individual's subconscious motivations.

Sexuality and other instinctual desires hold significant relevance within the context of dark Persuasion. Throughout history, mankind has been susceptible to manipulation as a result of primal sexual instincts. Sexual and pharmaceutical substances have long served as tools for subjugation and manipulation of societal masses.

What is happening at that location?

Recollection can be a deceptive phenomenon. In the event of two individuals observing a particular incident, it is highly likely that their recollections of said incident will vary. Individuals may recall it as an instance in which they were subjected to victimization. An alternative perspective could perceive it as an occasion that upheld impartiality for all parties concerned. The potential for memories to fluctuate and resurface over the course of a person's lifetime exists. Reflect upon the earliest recollection within your mental archives. Without a doubt, it will undoubtedly be a significant part of your early years. Does this memory evoke positive emotions or negative emotions? At times, it is the disagreeable memories that remain most prominent.

This tool will serve as a reliable means to discern situations in which you are being manipulated, persuaded, brainwashed, or deceived. By accessing this enigmatic subconscious system, one will attain the capacity to safeguard oneself. This is an intricate endeavor that necessitates extensive experimentation and the acquisition of significant expertise.

Guarding Against Manipulation

A considerable proportion of individuals fail to comprehend the fact that there is an orchestrated effort to manipulate and confuse us. We might experience a disconcerting instinct in our core that does not align with the speaker's words or feel compelled to comply with a request. The overwhelming majority react in ways that exacerbate misuse or succumb to the schemes of the abuser, potentially leaving us feeling insignificant and vulnerable, yet subsequently acquiescing to unacceptable behavior. If one were to have encountered a parent with manipulative tendencies, it might be more apt to perceive such an individual as an accomplice, as it is widely acknowledged.

Understanding your opponent is fundamental when dealing with a manipulator, employing knowledge that has become outdated. Being provided with the capability to identify these concealed bolts allows for deliberate response to covert manipulation. Comprehending their intentions in order to engage with you.

When individuals behave detached forcefully, what appears inactive or guarded is actually covert animosity. It can be readily demonstrated to what extent their behavior is conscious or unaware. To the individual in question, it is inconsequential. The effect is commensurate. Exhibiting an overly empathetic disposition exposes one to the recurring threat of being subjected to abuse. When an individual overtly or covertly attacks you, they are exhibiting aggression.

Manipulators are prevalent in various spheres, including households, educational institutions, places of worship, and professional environments. Additionally, manipulative individuals can be encountered in various locations.

What are some strategies utilized by the manipulator? Some are barefaced; others are more subtle: Some are undisguised; others are more nuanced:

Bullying. This approach exhibits a strong and resolute demeanor, and can be considered quite modest. The underlying message is, "If you fail to comply with my requirements, you will deeply regret it."

Sense of Obligation. This strategy incorporates the term "should:" It is advisable to perform this action in order to uphold a moral character. It is advisable that you attend to the concerns I have raised. You should. I am seeking repayment for the amount you owe me...

The underlying implication is that if one fails to adhere to societal expectations, they are considered morally questionable, untrustworthy, disloyal, and an inadequate partner, spouse, child, or friend.

Sarcasm or Cutting Humor. This is presented as a jest, and upon encountering the other person, he asserts, "You are excessively sensitive." Do you possess the capacity to humorously embrace the situation at hand? The underlying message is assertive and evident: "Conform to my expectations or I will verbally confront you."

Play the Victim. The individual who consistently orchestrates gatherings of pity and displays such profound sorrow such that you inadvertently caused harm once again (given that, ultimately, you are a merciless wrongdoer). In order to avoid feeling like an unfeeling wrongdoer, one must adhere to and fulfill the manipulator's requirements.

Sighing/Slamming/Banging/Driving Erratically. This overtly manipulative approach is designed to rebuff you. The primary message conveyed to you, as someone you hold in high regard, forcefully strikes the entrance, departs hurriedly, and abruptly applies the brakes, is as follows: "You have failed to fulfill my desires, therefore I will not engage in a meaningful conversation with you. Instead, I will express my contempt for you through my actions."

Guilt trips. Expressions such as,"Remarkable indeed, what great fortune you possess!" or, "Some benevolent caretaker allows him to extend his hours of activity as per his requirements. I regret your inclination towards manipulation. The remorseful individual possesses a profound understanding of how to exploit your vulnerabilities. If he were to perceive your concerns regarding displaying cruelty, he would utterly obliterate the value of that particular matter.

Showering Sentiments. This type of manipulator endeavors to deceive you through offerings of blessings or possibly by presenting unreasonable commendations. Beneath his generosity lie steadfast bonds of dedication, and in the event that one fails to respond with authenticity, severe consequences shall be faced.

Silent Treatments/Sulking/Pouting. These strategies represent ineffective yet forceful disciplinary approaches, aimed at addressing the unfavorable behavior exhibited by you. This level of manipulation presents such a challenge that the affected individual will exert every effort to uphold a strategic distance from them.

Intentionally Stalling. Do you ever find yourself needing to remain devoted indefinitely to your beloved? It can be asserted that he is consistently procrastinating. At that juncture, it is highly probable that you are dealing with an individual who intends to manipulate both you and the situation, albeit in a covert manner.

This summary lacks comprehensiveness, and the techniques for manipulating someone are as diverse as individuality. Ensure the completion of the task is executed in order to assert that the manipulator is capable of strategically customizing their manipulative techniques to suit the particular individual in question.

For what purpose do manipulators engage in manipulation? The two main factors are:

To exert control over the interrelation and additional context

To uphold a strategic distance from moral responsibilities

If you find yourself in an undesirable situation with a manipulative individual, do not despair. There are strategies available to safeguard your well-being and effectively manage your current interpersonal circumstances. The fundamental reason that must be understood is that the crucial aspect of self-insurance lies in comprehending one key segment.

Cease mandating the endorsement of others

A secondary point to consider is to avoid allowing others to define or label you. The primary means through which manipulation can be effective is if it is allowed or permitted. The manipulator has conducted an assessment of your character and is aware of your flaws. He acknowledges the necessity for you to engage with him in a manner that embodies legendary qualities such as forgiveness and conciliation. He will employ his tactics to exploit your weaknesses (and strengths) to his advantage.

The primary means of resolving this type of relational dynamic is to cease rumination on the implicit message he is attempting to convey to you. Here are a few techniques to employ upon oneself in order to effectively moderate the manipulative influence exerted by the manipulator.

Recognize the cunning strategies for what they truly are – methodologies to exert control over you.

Cease imposing the demand for the other person to alter. Grant him the freedom to exercise his inclination for manipulation, if that is his desire. Taking all factors into account, it is imperative to recognize that you should not manipulate others any more than they should manipulate you. Acknowledge and give up.

Stop guarding yourself. If you observe that you are beginning to experience a sense of protection, it is advisable to cease communication and depart.

Neutralize the manipulator's control over you. Cease your expectations regarding the resolution of his problems.

Anticipate the manipulator employing a range of strategies to manipulate you. When you cease succumbing to his manipulations, he will escalate the situation. Be readied.

I resolve to cease being a person who excessively accommodates others. Allow the other individual to remain discontented."

Stand firm. Please make an effort to remain unaffected by the burden.

The utilization of cognitive programming techniques for mental manipulation can potentially be advantageous in ethical circumstances, although it may entail potential hazards if handled inappropriately.

While some individuals utilize them for purposes of self-improvement, others do not hesitate to employ them, thereby putting you at risk. Endeavor to avoid allowing oneself to be manipulated. Continue reading to discover these methodologies!

III - Rapport

How many among us aspire to being highly regarded and more effectively remembered? In order to enhance comfort and optimize success at networking events? To enhance the overall success rate of one's romantic encounters. To foster stronger relationships with our colleagues and cultivate more meaningful friendships?

Natural Language Processing (NLP) affords us the capability to foster greater intimacy with others by eliciting their trust and cultivating affability. Commonly, individuals tend to engage with others who hold analogous convictions and perspectives. We derive satisfaction from the sense of shared understandings and mutual respect within our interactions with others. It fosters a shared comprehension, laying the foundation for cultivating a more profound camaraderie. The formation of an inner voice fosters the development of interpersonal connections, conveying the idea that we share commonalities despite superficial differences. The establishment of shared grounds fosters a sense of being listened to and comprehended, thereby fulfilling a profound social inclination ingrained within us through the course of communal existence. It cultivates a sense of intimacy as we endeavor to identify and emulate the admirable characteristics of others.

Humans and the remainder of our primate kin possess a component referred to as mirror neurons. These mirror neurons facilitate the observation of actions performed by others and evoke within us the sensation of experiencing those actions firsthand. These neurons are activated when we perceive actions resembling our own, facilitating the imitation of novel behaviors demonstrated by individuals whom we perceive to possess comparable physical capabilities. Humans possess an inherent genetic inclination to seek out familiar and reproducible actions in others, serving as a mechanism for acquiring new abilities and fostering trust. Hence, it is unsurprising that our subconscious mind detects instances of mirroring and subsequently elicits a response grounded in trust.

We can effectively utilize the trust-establishing impact of mirroring in our engagements with individuals. Instruction in the domains of communication and nonverbal cues frequently emphasizes the technique of mirroring the stance of our conversational partner. We are acquiring the skills to effectively utilize neurolinguistic programming techniques in order to establish a sense of trust with the individual. This phenomenon arises intrinsically when two individuals are deeply immersed in a mutually captivating interaction. It is also a factor that we can intentionally capitalize on as students of NLP.

Implementing mirroring techniques to establish rapport and foster trust is a straightforward task. In your forthcoming dialogue, make a conscious effort to observe and analyze the interlocutor's physical cues, linguistic choice, and nonverbal mannerisms. Adopt a discreet mirroring technique by emulating elements such as their body language, speech tempo, and intonation. When the other individual reclines in their chair, and you slowly adopt a similarly relaxed posture, it indicates a mutual understanding and shared perspective. Both of you are gradually growing at ease with the ongoing dialogue. When one responds to another person's usage of formal vocabulary by elevating their own level of formality, it greatly exemplifies a sense of respect and parity. These behavioral indicators serve as evidence of your active participation and focused attention towards the conversation, thereby eliciting a response of trust from the interlocutor.

In a parallel manner to our ability to harness mirroring as a means of capitalizing on natural language processing and fostering trust, we can evaluate the presence of mirroring as a means of exploiting natural language processing in order to gauge the level of involvement another individual demonstrates towards us. This information is instrumental in assessing the level of trustworthiness we can place in this individual during the present interaction. Due to the innate nature of mirroring during genuine engagement, the presence of mirroring from the interlocutor is typically indicative of their active involvement in the conversation and their desire to establish a rapport with you. A different approach would be that, in instances where an individual possesses an understanding of mirroring and chooses to practice it, this can be interpreted as an indication that there exists a sincere intention to establish a connection.

We have the ability to conduct simple tests in order to ascertain the presence of mirroring. To illustrate this point, consider making a minor alteration to your posture and observe whether the other individual gradually mirrors your new stance. Furthermore, experiment with gradually altering the pace of your conversation and observe whether the other individual adeptly adapts to this change. Decelerate your pace and observe whether they reciprocate by decelerating as well. Increase your pace, and observe if they join you on this journey. The response, or lack thereof, will serve as an indicator of their level of engagement in the conversation and significantly influence the extent of trust you place in them.

While the concept of mirroring is readily comprehensible and implementable, it boasts formidable capabilities in fostering and evaluating relationships. Take into account the potential to utilize this idiosyncratic aspect of NLP as a means to foster rapport in your upcoming discourse.

How to Keep Motivated

I strongly advise that you document everything that we have discussed in this chapter and store it in a secure location. This will facilitate your ability to reference it, preserving your focus and motivation as you progress on this journey.

Experience the discomfort arising from remaining in the present circumstances.

We collectively desire to steer clear of unpleasantness and discomfort.

And alteration brings forth a sense of unease. Pursuing our ambitions can entail difficulties; these difficulties may be so formidable that individuals may choose to forgo their pursuit.

I implore you to meticulously document and contemplate the immense suffering you endure as a result of persisting in your present circumstances. Please take a moment to consider the potential challenges that may arise if your current circumstances persist.

Harness the anguish you experience as a source of motivation for advancing.

Consider this: Your circumstances will remain unchanged if you fail to make any alterations. Perceive yourself as the ultimate authority in shaping your own destiny, recognizing that the sole agent capable of effecting transformative outcomes resides within oneself.

I kindly request that you reflect upon the potential outcomes that may arise from continuing to remain in your present circumstances.

Stay positive

It is important to take into consideration that the objectives you set for yourself should consistently be of a positive nature. It is prone to happen that individuals may unwittingly focus solely on what they wish to avoid rather than their genuine desires, resulting in a significantly unproductive approach.

Now, I implore you to recall the vividness of your aspirations and the exhilaration of realizing those aspirations, to possess whatever you desire.

In order to remain aligned with your goals, it is imperative to maintain the conviction that there exist avenues through which you can advance towards the realization of your desired life. It is essential to acknowledge the prospect of acquiring knowledge and gradually making progress.

It is imperative that you divert your attention towards devising strategies to overcome obstacles, and effectively striving towards the attainment of your objectives, instead of succumbing to the detrimental mindset of pessimism and disempowering beliefs, self-doubt, and negativity.

Train your mind to contemplate your conceptualization of triumph: what are your aspirations, where do you envision your forthcoming existence? What subject matter are you interested in acquiring knowledge about? In what manner do you aspire to cultivate personal development?

Directing your attention towards contentment rather than discontent will serve as a crucial determinant of your triumph.

Devoting attention to one's personal triumphs will serve as the true impetus for establishing objectives.

Think about how it is great to go through the process of achieving your goals. Envision the profound sense of pride that awaits you upon actualizing your aspirations. Allow yourself to experience the profound gratitude that emanates from embodying your utmost potential.

Embrace the forthcoming transformations in your life with enthusiasm! Contemplate the profound personal growth that awaits you as you navigate and triumph over the obstacles that lie ahead.

The subsequent section of the book is exclusively devoted to presenting straightforward NLP techniques designed to facilitate the attainment of your long-held aspirations, in an engaging and efficient manner.

Exercise 2: Grounding

This exercise serves as a commendable foundational practice, laying the groundwork for numerous subsequent NLP methodologies. By grounding yourself, you are promptly inducing a tranquilizing influence on both your physical and mental state. This will enhance your receptivity towards NLP exercises, thereby augmenting the likelihood of expedited and enduring transformation. It can further serve as a straightforward and efficacious method to induce a state of relaxation at one's discretion and in any location. In the event that you are experiencing a challenging morning at your place of employment, it would be advisable to momentarily close the door to your office and make preparations for promptly improving your state of mind.

Please commence by taking off your shoes and socks. Assume a standing posture with both feet firmly planted on the floor. If feasible, endeavor to carry out this exercise in an outdoor setting to enhance its relaxation benefits. Inhale and exhale deeply. Assume a position where your arms are relaxed and resting at your sides, while keeping your feet at a distance approximately equal to the width of your shoulders. Close your eyes. Envision, if you will, a state where you are firmly rooted to the earth, impervious to any forces that could disrupt or unsettle your equilibrium.

Gently flex your toes and envision them firmly anchoring you to the ground, providing you with stability. Maintain the extension of your legs while avoiding the complete immobilization of your knees. Take a deep breath, and as you exhale, purposefully endeavor to slightly lower your shoulders. Envisage the release of your inner strife and anxiety dissipating from your being, as you expel your breath.

After attaining a state of relaxation, direct your focus towards your lower abdominal region, precisely 2-3 inches below your navel. Gain awareness of the muscular tension present and observe how it sustains your upright posture. Recognize the profound sense of stability you have attained. I urge you to uncover your eyes and maintain a gentle and unwavering focus. Remind yourself of your profound state of relaxation and reinforce your ability to overcome any challenges that arise in life. Maintain steady and rhythmic respiration.

Engage in this exercise consistently on a daily basis for a brief duration, and you will gradually experience an innate sense of stability effortlessly. Please ensure that you periodically shift your focus to the area located beneath your navel. By adopting this approach, you are effectively instructing yourself to cultivate a state of tranquility, serenity, and composure whenever your attention is redirected to that specific area of your physique. After the passage of a few days, make an effort to sustain this state of relaxation and stability while you engage in ambulation. Through consistent training, you will acquire the ability to invoke a profound state of relaxation and self-assurance at will. This technique holds immense value in situations characterized by high pressure, such as job interviews or engaging in important discussions with individuals you hold in high regard.

www.ingramcontent.com/pod-product-compliance
Lightning Source LLC
Chambersburg PA
CBHW050246120526
44590CB00016B/2230